Dancing Through the Storm

Dancing Through the Storm

Reflections of a Black Woman During the Pandemic

Helen J. Gore

Charleston, SC
www.PalmettoPublishing.com

Dancing Through the Storm
Copyright © 2022 by Helen J. Gore

All rights reserved
No portion of this book may be reproduced, stored in a retrieval system, or transmitted in any form by any means—electronic, mechanical, photocopy, recording, or other—except for brief quotations in printed reviews, without prior permission of the author.

First Edition

Paperback ISBN: 978-1-63837-599-9
eBook ISBN: 978-1-63837-598-2

Table of Contents

Dedication vi

Part One: Family and Friends
1. My Daughter 3
2. My Mother 5
3. Remembering My Sisters 7
4. Two Brothers 9
5. A Tribute to Dad 11
6. My Family 13
7. Friends 15

Part Two: Four Different Sides of Me
1. The Insecure Side (To Be Invisible) 19
2. The Confident Side (Deep Within) 21
3. The Romantic Side (A Place in Your Heart) ... 23
4. The Impatient Side (Waiting! Trying to Be Patient) 25

Part Three: My Negative Views
1. A Date We Will Never Forget 29
2. Another Black Man Was Killed! 31
3. Divided We Fall 33
4. Stumbling Blocks 35
5. That Lady on The View 37
6. The Twilight Zone 39

Part Four: My Positive Views

1. A Better World 43
2. Cautiously Happy 45
3. Mothers 47
4. The World has Lost a Great Man 49
5. To Save the World 51
6. We Still Have Hope 53
7. Where Do Dreams Go? 55

Author Biography 57

Dedication

This book is dedicated to my awesome daughter who encouraged me and was the main source of my inspiration. Also, some family members and friends contributed to my decision to write this book of poems. Numerous events during the past 22 months have caused me to feel somewhat disillusioned. Therefore, I wrote several poems as a means of self-encouragement. I was also inspired when I listened to Amanda Gorman recite her poem at President Biden's Inauguration and I am extremely proud of her. Hopefully, some of my poems might serve as encouragement to family, friends, acquaintances, and other individuals who might share or appreciate my reflections.

PART ONE:
Family and Friends

My Daughter – Remarks

I was inspired to write this poem after observing the dynamic personality of my daughter! When we work as a team there is no limit to what we can accomplish. I am so grateful to have her as such a dedicated and thoughtful daughter. My daughter had a special bond with my mother because she always gave her genuine compliments and made her laugh. Therefore, my mother was always delighted to see her. I am also proud of her accomplishments as a devoted teacher, counselor, dean and learning specialist.

My Daughter

My daughter is unique and special in every way. I admire her essence each day.
Many individuals just don't understand. She has her own vision and follows her own plan.
She's not able to surrender to other people's roles. She's determined to pursue her own goals.
She's not worried about what other people think. She will dismiss their criticism without a blink.
It's not difficult for her to impress. But at the same time, she makes it clear that she's not taking any mess. An outstanding teacher, almost as influential as a preacher. Dedicated to helping family and friends. "I've got your back "is the message that she sends. Her main objective is to please. Her relentless efforts will never cease. Just sit back and take a seat. This young lady dances to her own beat. I know her determination will help her endure any complicated situations which are not pure. So, world look out and beware of her existence. She is going to conquer the world with her amazing charm and persistence.

My Mother - Remarks

I was so pleased to see my mother enjoy being the center of attention. We made sure that we gave her a big celebration starting with her 90th birthday. Unfortunately, she passed in October 2019 after struggling with several health issues. During the last two years of her life, we all went to see her as often as possible, but my younger brother and his wife made a special effort to travel from California to North Carolina several times. They tried to make sure that she had everything she needed. My niece who lives in Winston-Salem was especially helpful when my mother needed assistance. Also, my younger sister and her husband cared for my mother in their home during my mother's last year. She was always very wise and truthful and always gave all her relatives very helpful advice. She helped to raise her grandchildren as well as her great grandchildren. Memories of her will always be precious to all our family members and friends.

My Mother

My mother was so adorable, and I have to say, she always gave me good advice and encouraged me to pray. Her most famous words were "It's rough". We all had to agree that conditions throughout this world were tough. She was always willing to prepare my favorite dish. She enjoyed being able to grant anyone's wish. A few compliments could always make her laugh. She made me want to follow her humble path. No matter what you said, she would speak her mind. Sometimes her words did not appear to be kind. At family gatherings, mom loved to be seen. Everyone endeavored to make her feel like a queen. Her smile and wisdom were so inspiring. To make her happy was always worth trying. Thoughts of her will remain with us and remember this. Her warmth and kindness, we will forever miss.

Remembering My Sisters- Remarks

Two of my sisters have passed but I will always have wonderful memories of them to help ease the pain. Both of my sisters had daughters who I am proud of, and I am honored to be their aunt. I feel like a part of my sisters lives on in these two lovely ladies. They are always helpful and supportive, and I really appreciate them and their children. Both are wise beyond their years. My younger sister also had two sons and a grandson who has been very supportive. My oldest sister had one grandson and one granddaughter. I am very proud of all of them. I also have two sisters who I did not meet until later in my life. We do not communicate often but I am glad that they and their children are a part of my life.

Remembering my Sisters

We did not always get along, but we would always make up and admit when we were wrong. They were always lively and full of fun. Pursuing each task until it was done. Sometimes they gave comfort and support. Often just being helpful and a good sport. Their spirit will always be here. Pleasant thoughts of them will always be dear. Occasionally, there were heated discussions. So, we had to endure the repercussions. Still, we stood together for a common goal. Supporting each other was our role. They could be so warm and tender. When they believed in something, they would not surrender. I am so grateful for our connection and will never forget their love and affection.

Two Brothers- Remarks

I was inspired to write this poem because two of my brothers have such contrasting outlooks, even though they are both very supportive. I also have two brothers who I did not meet until later in my life. They are also very supportive, and I am glad that they are a part of my life. I do not communicate with them often, but it is always a pleasure and an enlightening experience when I am fortunate enough to communicate with them. They all have intelligent and talented children and spouses. I am proud of all of them

Two Brothers

I have a younger and an older brother. Neither one is like the other. Both are unique in their own way. A very important role in my life, they each play. No matter what predicament I face, both will help me to maintain my place. One is always so laid back and cool. The other brother insists that we follow the rule. One will say "Don't take a chance." The other will say" It's just a part of romance." Both were influential when I had a doubt. Always giving me the benefit of what they thought. One is mostly optimistic. The other mainly realistic. I am so glad they are a part of my life. Helping me to avoid unnecessary strife. No matter what obstacles my enemies might send, on my two brothers I can always depend.

A Tribute to Dad – Remarks

My Dad took so much pleasure in celebrating the holidays with his children, listening to oldies, and enjoying a delicious meal. He also enjoyed sports and was extremely excited about the accomplishments of Tiger Woods and the Williams sisters. He served in the U.S. Army for twenty years and served as a Capitol police for many years until he was promoted to serve as a Detective at the Capitol. He passed in November 2004. We miss him and think of him often.

A Tribute to Dad

He was always there when times seemed rough, letting us know that even though conditions were tough, we had someone we could depend on. All we had to do was pick up the phone. He helped us when we needed him the most. He was our financial and emotional supporter and host. Teaching us to appreciate music, sports, and history. Inspiring us to move on to our own victory. Sometimes we had to wait for hours for Dad to get dressed. But once he was finished, everyone was impressed. He loved seeing all his children together. He reminded us that with unity, any storm we could weather. He will always be in our heart. From our mind and thoughts, he will never depart. We will miss him, and we will never forget. His charm, his humor, and his mindset. We know that he will be watching over us from above like a lovely precious dove.

My Family- Remarks

I have family members who live in different states, but we always remember to communicate with each other and have often celebrated joyful occasions and gave comfort to each other on sad occasions. I appreciate all my nieces, nephews, siblings, in laws and other family members. This poem is dedicated to all of them.

My Family

My family means so much to me. I have so many nieces, nephews, and other family members who I rarely see. Still, I love, admire, and appreciate them all and I know that a significant connection can be made with just a single phone call. They are wise, full of life and fun, talented and dedicated. Their loyalty and support make me proud that we are related. Sometimes disagreements may cause some of us to be stressed. But God heals our anger, and we are forever blessed. Conflicts, resentment, and misunderstandings may arise. Nevertheless, that's not enough to destroy our family ties.

Friends- Remarks

I appreciate all my friends, but especially my close friends who have been there when I needed them the most. Marilynn, Hazel, Sharon, and Barbara are close friends who I have known and depended on for a long time. One of my dearest friends, Joyce passed in August 2020. I knew her ever since we went to elementary school together. We stayed in touch with each other and even though we did not see each other in the last years before her death, we always called each other and provided helpful advice when needed. I also appreciate the friends who I met in the hand dancing community. We are devoted to the joy of dancing. In addition, those friends who went out of their way to give me a ride home including one devoted Lyft driver who picked me up even in inclement weather. Unfortunately, Beverly, one of my friends from the hand dancing community passed away in June 2021. She was a kind and beautiful person and will be missed by many.

Friends

I have friends that I have known for many years. We have laughed a lot but also shared many tears. Some friends have passed and gone away, but I am glad that their spirit is still here to stay. Some of my closest friends are still here. They often listen to me and help ease my fear. I realize how important their friendship is and it will never end. Having their kindness and support, I can always depend. They always help me celebrate my birthday and any important date. They even remember the little things that I appreciate. Whenever I encounter an unfair attack, I know my friends will have my back. Even when I am worried and upset, they help me to make a decision that I will not regret. I hope they know that I also care. Whenever they need me, I will be there. I thank God each day for every special friend. They are precious gifts that only God could send.

PART TWO:

Four Different Sides of Me

The Insecure Side-Motivation

On various occasions, I have felt misunderstood and unappreciated which was the inspiration for this poem.

The Insecure Side (To Be Invisible)

I am aware of my surroundings, and I am so grateful that I can see. But when I am not acknowledged; does my existence seize to be? Often, I feel like people listen, but they don't understand. I am just trying to explain my opinion, not giving a command. My outlook might not matter to you but if you reflect for a minute, you might see my point of view. Like everybody else, sometimes I'm confused. That doesn't mean that I want to be abused. Just give me the respect that I deserve, and I will do the same for you. This gives all of us the opportunity to be fair and true. Many times, I wanted to speak up, but I was afraid. Have you ever felt that reluctance? Doesn't it make you feel sad? It is so easy to get lost in the crowd. But if one person notices you, doesn't it make you feel proud? There are so many beautiful and wonderful visions all around. Just like me, they only need to be found.

The Confident Side – Motivation

On rare occasions, someone will communicate with me or compliment me in a very positive manner. This encourages me to display more confidence and boldness.

The Confident Side (Deep Within)

Deep within, I am spontaneous and bold. A rare and magnificent person to behold! Do not underestimate me, don't you dare. "I didn't k now what I was missing", you will declare. My worth and value are more than you realize. Step back and look and you will see the prize. If you don't know, you better ask someone. You will find that I am amazing, and I am second to none. I am not bragging. I just want it to be known that a miracle happened on the day that I was born!

The Romantic Side – Motivation

My favorite hand dancing partner at the Elks Lodge was the inspiration for this poem.

The Romantic Side (A Place in Your Heart)

A place in your heart is good enough for me. Anything more, just wasn't meant to be. Even though my real feelings; I would like to confide. I try to hide them, but certain aspects are implied. I will just keep the fantasy alive. It contributes to my happiness and makes it thrive. Just know that my feelings are sincere. No matter how nonchalant I might appear. Sometimes the fantasy is better than the reality. It allows you to avoid any negativity. Just an embrace and a smile kept me captivated for a while. Just dancing, especially an intimate dance, turned out to be a significant part of romance. So many sentimental words have been spoken. I would like to think they were more than a token. When I remember some of the special moments that we did share, other occasions could not compare. Through good and bad times and all kinds of weather, I will always cherish the time we spent together.

The Impatient Side-Motivation

Sometimes people do not realize that they are taking you for granted. I guess that is why patience is a virtue.

The Impatient Side — (Waiting! - Trying to be Patient)

Waiting for you to say, "you are so wise". Whenever that happens, it will be a wonderful surprise. When I give you advice, I am only thinking of you. I am waiting for you to realize that I am not telling you what to do. Waiting for you to say, "without you I would not have won". This would let me know that you appreciate all I have done. I hope one day you will understand that being taken for granted was not something I would have planned.

PART THREE:

My Negative Views

A Date We Will Never Forget

January 6, 2021 is a date we will never forget. A dangerous and disrespectful tone was set. An entire year has come and gone. Yet the dreadful message still exists and has grown. Will the people involved in this destructive event be made accountable? Their crimes against our democracy are insurmountable. Do we need to change our justice system? Do we have to plead?

Will we be able to remove this evil seed? The harmful conspiracy theories are spreading at a very fast pace. Please God help us to overcome Satan's plan and win this race! The so-called patriots say that their violent actions were justified. The fact that their actions were senseless and unconstitutional cannot be denied. We appreciate the police officers who fought to defend our congressmen and our rights, and we feel their pain. Their deaths and suffering must not be in vain. We need to urge all elected representatives who believe in equality and justice to take a stand. Let them know that this is not a request, it is a collective command!

Another Black Man was Killed!

Another black man was killed, but hopefully it was not in vain. Even though he had to endure so much pain. So often black lives don't seem to matter. But at least this terrible predicament brings us together. A cold hearted and arrogant policeman thought he could ignore his victim's plea and disrespect a fellow human being even though the whole world could see. How many times will the deaths and suffering of black people be ignored? In our minds and hearts, these terrible incidents will forever be stored. To see a desperate man, cry out for his mom. I wish she could have reached out and protected him from harm. I can't breathe he declared, but his life was not spared. But God made sure that despite death, there was a victory. Twelve jurors decided on a justified guilty verdict that will go down in history. There's still a lot of work to be done and the whole justice system will have to be changed before the real and ultimate victory is won!

Divided We Fall

Divided we fall. This applies to not just some citizens, but all. With hatred and racism, we can never survive. With love and understanding, the whole world will thrive. Regardless of race, sex, or religion, justice, and fair play can eliminate division. Don't be blinded by jealousy and spite. Let the well-being of everyone be your plight. We should resolve to make unity our choice.

This commitment should be repeated by every voice. Corruption and greed are part of the predicament. Consider God's love. Let that be your sentiment. God has the whole world in his hands. Contemplate his wisdom, then follow his demands. Destroying and fighting each other is worse than any disease. Once we resolve our differences, these conflicts will cease.

Stumbling Blocks

From the depths of our soul, we struggle to survive. With the inner workings of our mind, we continue to strive. History repeats itself and we wonder why. Will we endeavor to find a solution or at least try? Should we dare to realize that what we thought was impossible can be transformed into something completely possible. Is this concept realistic, is it even plausible? Maybe once we understand that every obstacle is only a stumbling block, a positive and rewarding outcome should not be a shock. Each goal can be achieved, and we will see once we acknowledge that persistence is the key. With hope we can overcome despair and warn our enemies to beware. Never give up because victory is only a mindset away. The goals which we envisioned just might come true today.

That Lady on the View

I am always inspired when watching the View. I am also impressed by most of the ladies too.

But I was often enraged by one lady. Her attitude and thoughts were somewhat shady. She seemed to want to be the center of attention. No matter what subject the other ladies would mention. Most of her comments were so confusing. Some people even found her amusing. Her opinions were so unrealistic. She seemed to support people who were often sadistic. Maybe one day she will get a clue. At least we no longer have to listen to that lady on the View.

The Twilight Zone

I can't believe our world has sunk so low. There is so much room for compassion and empathy to grow. A liar, a conspiracy advocator, and a cheater. Is this the kind of person we wanted for our leader? No sense of decency or respect. Treating all women like an object. Ignoring the reality of death. This was such a brutal and dangerous path. Never displaying any remorse. An evil and insensitive force. Still so many say he's the best. What kind of crazy spell has he cast? Are his supporters experiencing the same delusion? Is that what made them reach such an unwise conclusion? His deeds were in the name of law and order, he would claim. What a disgraceful way to gain fame! Will God come to our defense against this vile and shameful nonsense? I am still praying that our society can survive, and honesty and intelligence can once again thrive. Hopefully with our new president we can all win and erase the former president's corruption and sin.

PART FOUR:

My Positive Views

A Better World

Gandhi's enemies tried to put him to the test. Even with fasting and prison, he still pursued his quest. Martin Luther King marched and prayed for peace. Criticism and beatings could not make him cease. Love your neighbors regardless of their race. You can still enjoy your individual space. If we all work together, there's no storm we cannot weather. If we insist on being divided, everyone will suffer, and relief will not be provided. I must confess that I am not happy with the stress. What about you? Would you like a better world too? Just start spreading love, that's all you must do. Remember the storm is passing over and our breakthrough is closer. A rainbow will appear giving us a sign that victory is near. I pray we can move forward after the fire. That's the kind of world I desire. Martin Luther King had a dream. I know he would be pleased if he knew we were all on the same team.

Cautiously Happy

Happiness can be achieved by just appreciating the little things. Meaningful activities are much better than dangerous flings. "Life is too short" someone said but I would rather be careful than do something that I will eventually dread. It is better to think about the potential consequences than to throw caution to the wind and eliminate all your defenses. A smile and a compliment from a very good friend. Dancing to a special song that you don't want to end. Invigorating music that energizes your soul. Soothing music that you might listen to while you stroll. A pleasant conversation preferably with a little flirtation. Eating my favorite dish is often my most desirable wish. A comedy or movie that makes you laugh helps pave the way for a pleasant path. Reading an informative book can enrich your mind. Valuable lessons you will most likely find. Happiness can easily be achieved. Just open your heart and it will be received. Maybe you have a favorite hobby you would like to share. Make sure you pick someone who will really care.

Mothers

Honor and respect your mother, God only gives you one. She is there to love and support you, rather you have lost or won. There are numerous opportunities we enjoy without a thought. Mainly because of the many battles she has fought. Although you may be impressed by certain individuals and the current trend, don't forget that your mother is probably your most dependable friend. Do not pass up the opportunity to give her praise. Her confidence and spirit you will surely raise. Even though some moms have passed and are no longer here, their loving memory can bring forth joy and yes, also, a tear. So, appreciate your mother while she is still alive. This kind of compassion will allow both of you to thrive. Make sure your actions are kind and sincere. When you look out for each other, you don't need to fear.

The World has Lost a Great Man

The world lost such a great man when we lost Mr. Sidney Poitier. There are so many wonderful things that I could say. I have admired him ever since I was very young. The list of his accomplishments is extremely long. Mostly I was impressed by the fact that he had very little formal education. Yet he taught himself to read and survive with relentless dedication. He made many people, especially black individuals extremely proud. The roles he played were meaningful and not just to please the crowd. Displaying such strength of character at such an early stage. Obviously, this caused some citizens to have a lot of rage. As a policeman in "In the Heat of the Night" he showed us that a black man could win the fight. As a black man in "Lilies of the Field", he illustrated what magnificent accomplishments good communication could yield. His roles as an actor and civil rights activist helped him to reach his goals. To make the world a better place and enrich our souls.

To Save the World

To save the world, what will it take? Our souls and livelihood are at stake. We cannot depend on our discretion. We must decide to go in the right direction. We all belong to the human race. Problems and hardships, we all must face. If we all just take the time to communicate and understand each other, our progress towards a peaceful existence could advance a little further. Bitterness and discrimination will always be an obstruction. This frame of mind will inevitably lead to destruction. God will lead us and if we follow, we can all look forward to a brighter tomorrow. So many people have been misled. If we peacefully interact with each other, our hunger for a harmonious world will be fed.

We Still Have Hope!

The world is not a perfect place, but we still have hope. Be grateful and maintain a positive attitude and realize that any problem we can face because we still have hope. Although, we can't do all the things we used to do, there are still so many privileges we can appreciate, not just a few. The sun still shines brightly, and we can rest and retire nightly. We can eat and drink and communicate with other people and let them know what we think. If flowers continue to bloom, we can renew our lives and overcome gloom. Therefore, we still have hope. God is still watching over and blessing us so let's not continue to fuss. We are all entitled to make a choice. So, let's thank God with an uplifting and resounding voice.

Where do Dreams Go?

Where do dreams go? Do they disappear just because someone says so? Are do they become lost in space, simply because they could not find a suitable place? Maybe all we must do is believe; so that eventually a confirmation we will receive. Just continue to have a positive point of view. Perhaps that's all you need for your dream to come true. Let your outlook continue to be bright. That's the only way you can win this fight. Remain optimistic and upbeat. Never ever accept defeat. Do not let your dream just fade away. Keep on believing and your dream will stay. Eventually your dream will come true, no matter what other people say or do. This is your vision, and you have the power. Keep working on your goal hour after hour. Be true to yourself and have no fear. This way your dream will never disappear.

Author Biography

I was born on September 24, 1950, in Arlington, Virginia on Fort Myer Army Base where my father was stationed serving in the army. My parents were John E, Gore and Olivia P. Gore. I attended Kimberly Park Elementary School located across the street from my home in Winston-Salem, North Carolina where I spent most of my childhood. After completing elementary school, I attended Paisley High School. One of my accomplishments was becoming a member of the National Honor Society. I graduated from High School and was accepted as a freshman at Hampton University. My major was English, and my minor was Journalism. I had a parttime job as a reporter during my junior year. I was fortunate to become roommates with a very intelligent and sociable young lady named Marilynn during my sophomore year. We became close friends and remained roommates throughout our junior and senior year. Marilynn and our friend Liz were very popular, so I was able to go to numerous parties with them. I was so happy when I was able to make the Dean's list.

After I graduated from Hampton, I went home to North Carolina where I worked as a preschool teacher at Martin Luther King Day Care Center for about one year, I decided to move to Washington, D.C. in search of better opportunities. I signed up with five temporary agencies and worked at a law firm, Geico and other companies. Finally, I was hired as a staff assistant for Senator Lloyd Bentsen from Texas. I worked there for eighteen years. I enjoyed being able to answer correspondence about civil rights issues. During this time, I met and married my husband, Edward on July 25, 1981. My daughter, Angela was born on August 6, 1982. She turned out to be one of the greatest joys of my life. Unfortunately, my ex-husband passed in 2007. We were divorced in 1993 but remained friends.

I enjoy every type of music including gospel, jazz, blues, love songs, oldies, and reggae. For a long period of time, music has always been a very important part of my life. I was a member of the church choir and the praise dance group. When I feel a little depressed, music is always a source of inspiration and encouragement. Also, dancing has always been my favorite hobby.

Before I retired in 2003, I worked as a Library Services Assistant at the Department of Treasury. After the tragedy of September 11, 2001, we were offered the opportunity to retire early. I decided to take advantage of this opportunity. Before I retired, I had the honor of writing articles for the Treasury Newsletter. Since I had planned to buy a condo, I decided to buy one after I retired. I served on the condo board for a short period until I had to step down when my father passed in November 2004.

I was appointed as the personal representative to handle my father's estate. There were many complications, but we were finally able to settle everything after about four years. Soon afterwards. I agreed to serve as the treasurer for my condo association at the request of the president of the association. There were many problems but, fortunately, there were some condo owners who expressed appreciation for my service and were very helpful and supportive. During this time, I often relieved stress by going hand dancing, to the casino and sometimes to amusement parks.

I finally sold my condominium in December 2019. I was looking forward to spending more time just enjoying myself. Unfortunately, we all were made aware of Covid 19 in March 2020. Since then, I have limited my activities to line dancing, free style, and praise dancing at home. I also enjoy communicating with friends and family and listening to inspirational sermons and just being grateful for God's mercy and blessings. I am currently living with my daughter and very grateful that we can support each other. She has been a special Ed teacher for several years as well as a counselor and dean. She is currently employed as a Learning Specialist. I am so proud of her. My daughter encouraged me to write during this period. As a result, I wrote this book of poems.

www.ingramcontent.com/pod-product-compliance
Ingram Content Group UK Ltd.
Pitfield, Milton Keynes, MK11 3LW, UK
UKHW022241230426
12048UKWH00018BA/1387